Author Credentials and Memberships

Affiliations

American Psychological Association (APA), 2022

Delta Epsilon Tau (DET): International Honor Society, 2011

Golden Key (GK): International Honor Society for Academics
and Leadership, 2011

Information Systems Audit and Control Association (ISACA),
2016

International Information Systems Security Consortium (ISC)^2,
2016

Institute for Internal Controls (IIC), 2016

Sigma Beta Delta: International Honor Society in Business,
Management, & Administration, 2014

Society for Industrial and Organizational Psychology
(SIOP), 2022

Upsilon Pi Epsilon: International Honor Society for Computer &
Information Science, 2010

Education

Doctor of Strategic Leadership

Master of Arts, Industrial & Organizational Psychology [Coaching and Consulting]

Master of Science, Information Technology [Computer/Digital Forensics]

Bachelor of Science, Information Technology

Occupational Associates, Network Engineering

Associates of Applied Science, Computer Information Systems

Table of Contents

Introduction

Guide to Facilitation is a short but comprehensive guide on what it takes to be an effective and successful facilitator. Being an effective and successful facilitator is paramount to many organizational decisions, including process improvements. Many organizational situations will require varying methods of approaching facilitation. There is no one particular approach to facilitation thus, it is known as an art and a science. Facilitation is an art because it requires strategies of the facilitator and science because of the elements of facilitation that can be repeatable (Elledge et al., 2019). In addition to the content on facilitation, the appendix includes a facilitation quiz, a facilitator evaluation form, and a candidate employment negotiation strategy.

Learning Objectives

The learning objectives of this facilitator guide are to provide a platform for facilitators to understand what the criteria are for effective facilitation. The objectives will focus on facilitator competencies, skills, experiences, and conflict resolution approach. Additionally, the objectives will provide tools, resources, and strategies for effectively facilitating meetings. Overall, the learning objectives will summarize the practical application of facilitation in any organization.

Agenda

The facilitator's agenda is to support the organization and/or participants in solving problems or improving processes (IAF, 2018). Thus, the agenda is based on the needs of the organization and its participants rather than the facilitator's desire.

Facilitator Competencies

To be an effective facilitator includes having certain knowledge, skills, and abilities for facilitation. These elements factor into the competencies needed by effective facilitators. The professional organization that promotes and supports facilitation, the International Association of Facilitators (IAF), outlines 6 major competencies for effective facilitation. They are as follows:

1. Create Collaborative Client Relationships
2. Plan Appropriate Group Processes
3. Create and Sustain a Participatory Environment
4. Guide Group to Appropriate and Useful Outcomes
5. Build and Maintain Professional Knowledge
6. Model Positive Professional Attitudes as a Process Facilitator

These competencies which were developed by the IAF focus on the skills, knowledge, and behaviors that contribute to facilitation success in a varying number of environments (IAF, 2018). Each of these competencies has several subcomponents that lead to building relationships, managing time, displaying interpersonal skills, recognizing diversity and inclusion, and facilitating with clarity. In addition to these, the competencies describe managing group conflict, evoking group creativity, acting with integrity, and creating trusting relationships (IAF, 2018). Since facilitators perform duties such as these, guidelines for the work that they perform is critical to facilitator effectiveness. Additionally, facilitation skill development is critical to the performance of a facilitator. Competencies that focus on facilitation skills assist with navigating through the process, the approach to learning and planning, and facilitator neutrality (University of Kansas, n.d.).

Facilitator Skills

A facilitator is often known as someone who hosts meetings, conducts training, and leads team-based discussions (Bacal, 2019). However, the role is more in-depth than what most believe. A facilitator is also similar to a coach and a consultant. However, their primary role is to manage the information as it is exchanged between the other parties (Bacal, 2019; Elledge et al., 2019). Since facilitators manage information exchange, they must possess certain characteristics. There are quite a few characteristics that a facilitator must have to be successful. Of these characteristics, the ones that I see as the most important are:

- Asking rather than telling
- Initiating conversation
- Asking for opinions
- Listening without interrupting
- Self-confidence
- Persuasive
- Coaching style

Facilitators with these characteristics are vital to facilitating and managing relationships with clients. Clients would rather have a facilitator that asks questions, value opinions, exhibits confidence, and listen without interruption (Bacal, 2019). In addition, facilitators with a coaching style can be effective at initiating conversations and can be rather persuasive, with a focus on guiding teams. Facilitating can be a difficult role to perform but these characteristics along with role competencies can make that task easier. The role of a facilitator can be a referee, or a coach and they are expected to be prepared for anything that could happen, set guidelines, and be active listeners (Feldberg-Dubin, 2021). Groups and teams often rely on the skills and experience of a facilitator. As part of being prepared, facilitators must be able to adapt to changing situations.

Facilitator Meetings

In facilitating meetings, a lot of organizations, mine included, tend to conduct meetings that give out orders, provide a directive way of doing things, and allow little time for idea generation among participants. Running a meeting can be similar to an autocratic approach to

conducting meetings rather than a democratic approach.
Approaching a meeting from a facilitation perspective
presents the opportunity for creativity, idea sharing,
neutrality, and engaged participation (Linabary, 2020). The
facilitation approach to a meeting mirrors the democratic
style as it encourages the freedom to generate ideas.
Additionally, when leaders "run" meetings as opposed to
facilitating them, there is often a decrease in clarity, and
participants could be less prepared. Facilitators should
avoid running meetings and focus more on facilitating to
give all team members opportunities to share their ideas.
They should also support criteria that promote asking open
questions, waiting on responses, active and careful
listening, and flexibility.

Facilitator Strategy

Facilitation, as research suggests, requires
individual skills and is an art for implementing and
improving practices (Ritchie et al., 2020). Facilitating is not

training or teaching, although facilitators do employ elements of both. When facilitating groups, the overall goal of the facilitator is to be effective. Human factors such as personal behaviors and perspectives play a significant role in group dynamics. Facilitation rests upon not just what the organization needs, but also what the people in the organization need (Cserti, 2019). Thus, in organizations in which there are a lot of strong opinions and sometimes individuals that do not respect the perspectives of others, the art of facilitation is paramount. Some of the guidelines suggested by experts to facilitate effectively are:

- ***Asking open questions*** – This strengthens dialogue and provides multiple perspectives.

- ***Wait for participant response*** – Waiting a brief moment for participants to respond to any questions asked would allow them some thought before speaking.

- ***Careful listening*** – Listening carefully would help to understand the crux of the questions.

- ***Active Listening*** – The facilitator who listens to participants more and talks less, helps to encourage participant engagement and idea generation.

- ***Flexibility*** – Being flexible is extremely critical for facilitators because there are variances in every facilitation event.

When considering facilitation in organizations, needs are important, and establishing the criteria for resolving the types of problems that are an organizational concern (Ritchie et al., 2020). Tools and resources used by facilitators are additional impacts on facilitation.

Virtual Facilitation

Virtual meetings are often more difficult to facilitate than in-person meetings. Thus, the role of the facilitator can become more difficult when navigating the facilitation process with virtual means (Middleton et al., 2021). Body language is often difficult to recognize and tone and emotions are not easily recognized in the environment. As such, there are tips and guidelines to use that can help facilitate virtual settings and make meetings more productive and/or effective. The paragraphs that follow will provide some of these guidelines that facilitators can use for resources for effective virtual facilitation.

How to Optimize Virtual Meetings

In a recent study, neurologists have suggested key areas of focus for optimum virtual meetings. These areas are for the optimization of virtual meetings on the Zoom platform. The following are recommended tips for virtual meetings in Zoom (Avitzur, 2021):

Adjusting zoom settings. This involves using emojis, suppressing background noises, using a name, etc. to allow for fewer interruptions.

Using shortcuts. Particularly for rapid muting and unmuting, users are advised to use Alt + A (Windows) or Command+Shift+A (Mac).

Maintaining eye contact with participants. This helps to keep participants engaged in the meeting.

Turning on video. Allows you to recognize engaged participants and the ability to observe some facial expressions and body language.

Zoom cueing. This allows for the recognition of raised hands and conversations in the chat room.

Facilitate and take notes. The facilitator records the sessions and also takes notes during the live meeting.

Breakout sessions. For longer meetings with different areas of focus, it is often beneficial to have breakout meetings in smaller groups that promote activities and fun.

Devoting time to presentations. It is always beneficial to reserve time to present presentations and other content that focus on meeting objectives.

Using polls. The use of polls is useful for breaking the ice, such as presenting questions that focus on the primary areas of discussion.

Using polls to seek consensus. Polls can also be used to see the support or **perspectives** of the meeting participants.

The authors of this article suggest that these tips can help take the monotony out of meetings, foster engagement, and create a path for optimizing virtual meetings using the Zoom platform (Avitzur, 2021). While these tips were specifically for virtual meetings using Zoom, these (or similar) tips can also be helpful on other virtual platforms.

Running a Great Virtual Meeting

In another article, the authors focus on the criteria that it takes to run an effective virtual meeting. An interesting point about virtual meetings that these authors discuss is the tendency of meeting participants to regard virtual meetings as opportunities to work on other tasks (Frisch & Green, 2020). It is also noted that virtual meetings can lead to a select few speakers dominating the conversating with no feedback from other meeting attendees. The authors suggest there are ways to prevent people from focusing on other tasks during the meetings and the domination of the conservation by a minimal number of participants. Here are some suggested takes for optimizing virtual meetings (Frisch & Green, 2020):

Use video. This helps to personalize the conversation and allow observations to take place.

Provide an audio dial-in option. This would be helpful to people that have limited access to the meeting; they would still be able to chime into the proceedings.

Test the technology before the meeting starts. This would prevent meeting delays due to technical malfunctions of equipment, audio, and video.

Check for visible faces. The conversations can be more engaging and body language can be observed if the participants' cameras are on and capturing faces.

Stick to meeting basics. The objectives of the meeting are critical to maintaining the scope of the virtual meeting discussion.

Minimize presentation lengths. Minimizing the lengths of the presentations, remaining in scope, and avoiding too much time on a particular topic.

Break the ice. It is always a good thing to break the ice because that often puts minds at ease.

Assign a facilitator. This person should guide the discussion, keeps the conversation in scope, and should be assigned before a meeting starts.

Call on people. Calling on people helps to get everyone to participate in the conversation, in some cases, keeps participants alert.

Capture real-time feedback. Capturing feedback can be facilitated by polling the participants during the meeting.

Tackle tough issues. The facilitator or meeting host should use the virtual platform to discuss even controversial topics. Some conflicts now may lead to opportunities for success later.

Practice. It is also a clever idea to practice virtual meetings and provide feedback on the experience.

These are some of the suggested guidelines to facilitate virtual meetings with no specific platform in mind. The authors contend that the guidelines are vital to virtual meetings when the choice or availability for in-person meetings is not feasible (Frisch & Green, 2020).

Facilitator Tools and Resources

For facilitation to be effective, the appropriate tools and resources must be used by the facilitator (Seeds for Change, 2020). Facilitators use tools and resources that help to improve organizational processes, change management, conflict resolution, and other areas that have potential impacts on the mission of an organization. The choice of these tools is dependent on the skills of the facilitator, the dynamics of the group, the topics of the discussions, and the overall agenda. All of these choices for tools and resources would be considerations for facilitators planning and implementing strategies in organizations. Some tools that could work in either situation are brainstorming, mingling, and trust-building.

Brainstorming

Brainstorming is a tool that can be used by facilitators to encourage thought processes among extrovert and introvert group members (Gurchiek, 2017). Using this resource, each participant cast out ideas for solving problems, they are documented and then discussed. As a facilitator, it is useful to encourage everyone to have at least one idea to brainstorm and emphasize how critical it would be for varying input. Brainstorming starts with the unstructured sharing of ideas and topics. When brainstorming ideas are represented visually, such as on a whiteboard, they can be used as mind mapping to see how the ideas fit the problematic situation (Lee, 2019). Mind maps can be used to enhance brainstorming ideas and generate discussions to formulate common connections or rule out ideas for submission. So, in a facilitator's approach to the use of brainstorming, mind mapping could be used as a joint effort.

Mingling

Mingling is a good facilitator tool as it allows people who are strangers to get to know something about each other and created workplace happiness (Sekhon & Srivastava, 2018). One way for a facilitator to use mingling is through the use of a "speed dating" format. In this format, people are assigned a partner to have a dialogue with for short periods. During this time, they as each other questions about their life, career, education, and other background information. A signal is given, and each person is seated with a new partner to follow the same process for communication. This is a quick way to pick up just some things about a person. Mingling using the "speed dating" strategy would provide a simplified overview of participants when the focus is on information gathering with time constraints. Mingling would be a critical step for my approach to facilitation and provide a path to cultural discoveries and trust-building.

Trust Building

Mingling can be the first step to trust-building in some situations (Sekhon & Srivastava, 2018). Additionally, trust-building as a facilitator tool can be accomplished using activities so as games, problem-solving activities, and regular meetings. Games and activities that increase fun help to generate trust. Problem-solving activities, such as puzzles and riddles, can also be effective when a facilitator wants to build trust. Trust building from meetings is often a result of people spending a lot of time together. The more meetings that people attend together, the more they get used to each other and their perspectives, and the more likely trust will be created and promote successful facilitation (Mroz et al., 2018). This is another critical aspect of the use of a facilitation tool that facilitators can employ in their organizations to build trust and facilitate effectively.

Conflict Resolution

All organizations require personnel on staff employed that can assist with and manage conflict resolution. As a facilitator for meetings and events in organizations, strategies such as observing body language, remaining neutral, and intervening only when necessary can be effective. Using these guidelines as a practice can help keep the focus on facilitating the successful elements of the process. Additionally, practicing these strategies can not only reduce conflict but also assist with resolving and managing conflict. Conflict will always arise in environments with opposing perspectives on a topic and a facilitator can use techniques to resolve the conflict that is moving toward negative implications (Curriculum Leadership Institute, 2017). There are many other avenues that a facilitator can approach to resolve conflict. Every situation, conflict type, and individual behavior is handled in diverse ways.

One of the other avenues is using a system called *Dispute System Design*. The Dispute System Design (DSD) is a system that was designed by experts to help manage a resolved conflict (Martinez & Smith, 2020). The experts involved in this design were primarily consultants, educators, and subject matter experts. They developed the DSD process as a means to help leaders and facilitators resolve conflicts using streamlined methods. Rather than reinventing the wheel for facilitation, this system can be used as one tool for effective conflict resolution. As facilitators responsible for conflict resolution, conflict is considered from a positive perspective as well as a negative perspective. This means that facilitators have to encourage the team to focus on positive conflict and the good impacts it could have on the organization. Encouragement of conflict is an empowering factor among teams, and it increases enthusiasm, engages the team in stronger collaboration activities, and it encourages challenges to

authority.

If conflict among teams is always considered

negative and there is no focus on the positive, the

opportunity for increased collaboration is not realized

(Humphrey et al., 2017). Decision-making often requires

some conflict, challenges to authority, and some team

disagreements; these all allow the team time to spend

together defining problems and solutions (Humphrey et al.,

2017). Teams willing to be innovative and focused on

working through conflict and using it to resolve issues in

organizations are paramount to high-team performance.

Since conflict brings about the need to have further

discussions among teams, it is necessary to assess tasks. All

of these suggestions and guidelines would be a part of a

facilitator's toolbox for managing resolution.

Conclusion

The greatest concept for a facilitator to understand about facilitation is the necessity of the role (Elledge et al., 2019). As a facilitator, the role must be viewed as a medium to champion success. Acting as a liaison between the organization and the staff is a pertinent function. Facilitation must take place using a neutral stance with a focus on the needs of the team and organizational objectives (Elledge et al., 2019). As a general rule for facilitation within the organization, some primary areas of focus are:

- Striving to remain as neutral as possible

- Encouraging participants to provide input to discussions

- Creating methodologies for conflict resolution

- Guiding the team in the use of mind mapping and brainstorming

- Remaining focused on goals and objectives

- Requesting feedback from participants

In the organization, one of the most important things to understand about facilitation is the need for intervention and improvement (Metz et al., 2020). Facilitation helps intervention and improvement by meeting and discussing things that matter. As a facilitator conducting the event, neutrality is important. The facilitator does not take sides in the meetings, nor does he/she dominate the discussion. The facilitator also carries the responsibilities of a referee to de-escalate conflict and keep meetings on track and within scope (Linabary, 2020). This helps the organization stay connected with the objectives and maintain direction towards goals. Ultimately, a final approach to facilitating meetings in organizations should center on a total team-building effort.

References

Avitzur, O. (2021). Neurologists on how to optimize virtual

meetings: 10 tips to zoom like a pro. *Neurology*

Today, *21*(14), 10-11.

Bacal, R. (2019). *The Role of The Facilitator -*

Understanding What Facilitators Really DO!

Retrieved from:

http://work911.com/articles/facil.htm

Cserti, R. (2019). *How to improve your facilitation skills*

(and be a great facilitator). Retrieved from

https://www.sessionlab.com/blog/facilitation-

skills/#facilitation-skills.

Elledge, C., Avworo, A., Cochetti, J., Carvalho, C., &

Grota, P. (2019). Characteristics of facilitators in

knowledge translation: an integrative

review. *Collegian*, *26*(1), 171-182.

Feldbcrg-Dubin, A. (2021). *Top 11 skills of an effective*

facilitator. The Design

Gym. https://www.thedesigngym.com/top-11-skills-effective-facilitator/

Frisch, B., & Greene, C. (2020, March). What it takes to run a great virtual meeting. In *Harvard Business Review. https://hbr. org/2020/03/what-it-takes-to-run-a-great-virtual-meeting.*

Gurchiek, K. (2017). Extroverts and introverts: How to get the best work from both. *HRNews,* Retrieved from https://www.proquest.com/trade-journals/extroverts-introverts-how-get-best-work-both/docview/1860133870/se-2?accountid=14376

Humphrey, S. E., Aime, F., Cushenbery, L., Hill, A. D., & Fairchild, J. (2017). Team conflict dynamics: Implications of a dyadic view of conflict for team performance. *Organizational Behavior and Human Decision Processes, 142, 58-70.* doi:10.1016/j.obhdp.2017.08.002.

IAF (2018). *Core Facilitator Competencies*. Retrieved

from https://www.iaf-

world.org/site/sites/default/files/Revised%20IAF%2

0Core%20%20Competencies%20-

%20December%206%202021.pdf

Lee, L. (2019). *Ideastorming for innovation*. Retrieved

from

https://www.lilaandcompany.com/blog/2019/6/19/id

eastorming-for-

innovation#:~:text=One%20of%20the%20best%20

ways,them%20to%20find%20the%20gems.

Linabary, J. (2020). Facilitating group meetings. *Small-

Group Communication*. Retrieved from

https://smallgroup.pressbooks.com/chapter/meeting

s/

Martinez, J., & Smith, S. (2020). *Dispute system design:

Preventing, managing, and resolving

conflict*. Retrieved from

https://papers.ssrn.com/sol3/papers.cfm?abstract_id
=3658572

Metz, A., Burke, K., Albers, B., Louison, L., & Bartley, L.
(2020). *A Practice Guide to Supporting
Implementation.*

Mroz, J. E., Allen, J. A., Verhoeven, D. C., & Shuffler, M.
L. (2018). Do we really need another meeting? The
science of workplace meetings. *Current Directions
in Psychological Science, 27*(6), 484-491.

Ritchie, M. J., Parker, L. E., & Kirchner, J. E. (2020). From
novice to expert: a qualitative study of
implementation facilitation skills. *Implementation
science communications, 1*(1), 1-12.

Seeds for Change. (2020). *Facilitation tools for meetings
and
workshops* [PDF]. https://seedsforchange.org.uk/too
ls.pdf

Sekhon, S. K., & Srivastava, M. (2018). Conquering

workplace loneliness individual or organization

accountability. *Human Resource Management

International Digest.*

University of Kansas (n.d.) *Section 2. Developing

Facilitation Skills. Community Toolbox.* Retrieved

from: https://ctb.ku.edu/en/table-of-

contents/leadership/group-facilitation/facilitation-

skills/main

Appendix A: Facilitation Quiz

1.   The focus of a facilitator is to
_______________________________.
  a.   change the organizational structure
  b.   teaching employees
  c.   taking sides during a dispute
  d.   assess the needs of the organization

2.   Which of these describe a characteristic of a
facilitator?
  a.   change manager
  b.   neutrality
  c.   dispute instigator
  d.   trainer

3.   Facilitators are only necessary for large groups.
(True or False)
  a.   true
  b.   false

4.   Do facilitators need to be concerned with positive
and negative conflict?
  a.   Yes, both provide opportunities for
       discussion
  b.   No, there is no point in recognizing positive
       conflict
  c.   No, all conflict is negative

5.   Which of these items strengthens the facilitation
process? (Choose all that apply)
  a.   active listening
  b.   taking sides in disputes
  c.   avoiding discussions

d. remaining neutral

6.   What should a facilitator do if a conflict arises between meeting participants? (Check all that apply)
   a. Avoid rushing to judgment
   b. Intervene immediately
   c. Choose which side of the argument to support
   d. Assess the situation before acting

Appendix B: Facilitator Evaluation Form
(For Use After a Facilitation Event Has Occurred)

1. Did the facilitator listen to the meeting or event participants?

   Yes

   No

   Unsure

2. Was the facilitator empathic to others?

   Yes

   No

   Unsure

3. Did the leader focus on the needs of the organization and its staff?

   Yes

   No

   Unsure

4. Was there any weakness noted in the facilitation?

   Yes

   No

Unsure

5. Did the facilitator practice persuasive tactics to influence the group?

Yes

No

Unsure

6. Did the facilitator outline measurable goals?

Yes

No

Unsure

7. Did the facilitator appear to have foresight into future outcomes?

Yes

No

Unsure

8. Was the facilitator a steward for the topics of discussion?

Yes

No

Unsure

9. Was the facilitator committed to finding solutions to

issues?

Yes

No

Unsure

10. Did the facilitator focus on building communication

among the group members?

Yes

No

Unsure

Appendix C: Employment Strategies for Candidates (The "Take the Carrot" Principle)

Introduction

In the world of work and employment, many elements exist that explain the relationship between the employer or representative and the employee. Oftentimes, people view this relationship as a one-way relationship. The Employer (representative/boss) tells you what to do and sometimes how to do it. This is a primitive way of thinking in present times. The employer issues a task and coerces the employee to complete this task by offering some form of award or, in some cases, consequences for not completing the task efficiently, effectively, or expeditiously.

I propose that candidates sell their best self, present evidence (accomplishments, credentials, etc.), and "take the carrot". Take the carrot is my advice to candidates for leveraging their best self, presenting quality to an organization, and landing in the driver's seat of employment expectations. It is a known fact that the key to landing a job originates with the ability to catch the employer's eye and peak his/her interest. Resumes, which include industry certifications, degrees, skills, and accomplishments are all part of these "attention getters". There are many different ways to write and format a resume, but there are certain elements in resumes that "sell" and also some elements that land the resume in the pile with no further review.

Resumes

Most people tend to follow the traditional resume formats that have been around for ages. These resumes include objectives, work experience, education, skillsets, references, etc. There are a few of these items that are practically irrelevant in today's technology-based job searches. Objectives really don't have good selling points to employers anymore. Employers are looking for people who can actually perform the job that is being advertised.

Objectives only tell an employer what a particular

candidate's goal or objective is from the candidate's

perspective.   Since most people have some goal or

objective, it is easy for employers to disbelieve stated

candidate objectives. Objectives are for the candidate's use

and do little to help the employer or company. Instead, a

summary of accomplishments has more value to the

employer. These accomplishments can replace objectives

on a resume and give the hiring manager an arena to focus

on and closely match the candidate to ongoing job

requirements.

Industry Certifications

Industry certifications do hold a certain level of

prestige in several industries. Many positions require them

to some extent, especially in fields such as business,

medical, information technology, and many others. I see

the value that certifications bring when a person put in the time and focus to really learn the material. I also see

negative implications when people just study enough

material to pass the exam. Additionally, I see a lot of

"coaching" programs to pass certification exams, but

minimum efforts are put into understanding the concepts.

The downside to this is people often forget the theory

behind the teachings of the field which could negatively

impact the focus on the crux of the job.

College Degrees

The value of college degrees is often stated to be a

diminished product. Many are opting to go for industry

certifications or other credentials instead of degrees.

However, I will always support the attainment of degrees

because academically, I support the idea that more

knowledge can be gained by bundling the ways of learning.

I would never recommend to anyone not to pursue an

accredited college degree of any type. The world has

changed so rapidly, and I genuinely believe that there is a

college program available for every type of learner. There are programs available for people who hate math, have difficulty reading and interpreting, or simply don't want to write papers. A program in some form awaits everyone who has a desire to have success, even when they prefer to be just small business owners.

Skill and Knowledge Drivers

Both industry certifications and degrees are supplements to skill achievement. There is value in them all, but the large benefit to organizations is that each of these potentially brings sustainable value to organizations. Knowledge management is a pertinent part of understanding the skills of individuals and the needs of organizations. Knowledge management is connected to some of the key drivers of organizational success and its primary focus is on people, their experiences, their training, and their skills. Some of these drivers are knowledge as assets, innovations, sources, and resources. Collectively, these drivers promote interest in the additional creation of knowledge, the value of people, and the continuous development of the organization's overall knowledge base.

Accomplishments

Accomplishments are particularly good additives to today's resumes. They can replace areas of the resume such as the Objectives and goals. Everyone has goals and objectives, but what value do these goals provide for an organization? Goals on resumes are often based on "cookie-cutter" approaches to resume creation processes. Accomplishments tell the employer what the candidate has already done and how this could potentially be an appropriate fit for a role. Accomplishments are strong drivers that allow the candidate and/or employee to truly "take the carrot".

The principle of "Take the Carrot" is a phrase that I created in 2012 while taking a university management course in a doctorate program. Don't be guided (or misguided) by what others think you are worth. Know your worth, establish your boundaries, and decide how you want to proceed in the workforce. An individual's ability to meet job-related criteria and exercise their abilities is much more crucial to the employer than someone who wants the paycheck but is not confident in his/her abilities. Take the Carrot!